Credit goes to
the team of designers,
photographers, cartoonists,
and editor Dean Goodluck
at the publisher: D'Moon

Copyright ©D'Moon
third edition, 2nd print: 2021
ebook edition: 2017
all rights reserved
except for reader comments and
poems & quotes not by LuCxeed

ISBN: 978-1-933187-96-9

Slight variations may occur
as part of the print-on-demand process
since each book is manufactured in its entirety.

Your feedback is most welcome ~
publisher@worldculturepictorial.com

Introduction

A ten-year journey
of Reading and Reflection,
sparkling with
knowledge and wisdom,
humour and diligence.

To thank the ever-appreciated
blessings, here comes
Four Steps Wiser,
leaping from on-line to off-line,
into fine-art quality press.
Enjoyable everywhere.

Each entry is a glimpse
as an invisible window
to technology's surprising
advancement (car outruns
bullet), amazing news
or character (Elvis was drafted
on Christmas holiday; 39
countries on all 7 continents
dance with Matt), or, goings-
on anywhere geographically
(the vow of a young king of a
nation on very high land,
three-day gasoline-free race);

in the time space, life in
century-old convent is on-
going, embracing modern life
with "modernity", fascinating!
Each entry offers a link to
relevant, stunning photos
or further online exploration.

Layer by layer, no spoilers.

Gentle hearts touched,
touching comments jotted.
Millions of readers have
dropped by, thousands have
written messages (some of
which come along in print) to
share feelings and knowledge
(car has wings to fly) or
simply tell they've been here
and enjoyed the read.

Wonderful experience and
learning - regardless the
happenings are awesome
or absurd. Readers' thoughtful
comments are truly encouraging
and half-way testimonials to
bring these books to more
people as the famed do many
other books.

Another uniqueness
of Four Steps Wiser
is to bring classic poems
into modern life. Poetry lives
beyond literature, and poets
are beyond masters of languages.
Classic poems also tell stories.
Poets live their lives and
have fantasies just as we do,
as expressed in witty and
humorous poem A Strange
Wild Song by Lewis Carroll -
"He thought he saw a Buffalo
 Upon the chimney-piece:
 He looked again,
   and found it was
 His Sister's Husband's Niece.
 'Unless you leave this house,'
   he said,
 'I'll send for the police!'

 He thought he saw
   a Rattlesnake
 That questioned him
   in Greek:
 He looked again,
   and found it was
 The Middle of Next Week.
 'The one thing I regret,'
   he said,
 'Is that it cannot speak!' "

We are created with vision
without limitation unless
limited by closed ears
to learn less.

Each volume offers around
100 invisible windows waiting
for you to open – enjoy the
fresh air, true stories from far
beyond horizon and time zone.
In "Speech", Mark Antony
attends his friend Julius
Caesar's funeral and talks
about an ambitious yet self-
claimed honourable man.
"Friends, Romans,
countryman, lend me your
ears" (Shakespeare), shall we?

We are saying goodbye to
yesterday, to last year,
and the near past seems to
never willingly part.
Our step forward or backward?

*World Culture Pictorial®

Publisher's Note

"Nature's law puts everything in order, holds everybody together. Mankind has been well taken care of: Nature supplies All to All" ("One Step Wiser"). Beautiful simplicity! To which great classic poems are dedicated, as here one of Samuel Taylor Coleridge's–

"To Simplicity
O! I do love thee, meek Simplicity!
For of thy lays the lulling simpleness
Goes to my heart, and soothes each small distress--
Distress tho' small, yet haply great to me!
'Tis true, on Lady Fortune's gentlest pad
I amble on; yet tho' I know not why,
So sad I am! but should a friend and I
Grow cool and miff, O! I am very sad!
And then with sonnets and with sympathy
My dreamy bosom's mystic woes I pall;
Now of my false friend plaining plaintively,
Now raving at mankind in general:
But whether sad or fierce, 'tis simple all,
All very simple, meek Simplicity."

Nature's Simplicity guides steps into a new year –
Good luck!

Dean Goodluck

Contents

Beginning
Copyright
Title Page
Introduction
Publisher's Note
Table of Contents

Section 1

2008/10/12
Poem in Art
"Over Earth and Ocean,
with gentle motion..."
- Percy Bysshe Shelley

2008/10/13
Tech vs Ocean
Fishing machines fast
fishing nets vast

Four Steps Wiser - WcP Reading & Reflection Vol. 04

Contents

2008/10/14
Sun unusually quiet
no observed sunspots
in 200 days

2008/10/15
unpleasant
25% of North Pole
Arctic naked without ice

2008/10/16
"I was like a boy playing
on the sea-shore..."
- Isaac Newton

2008/10/17
Queen Elizabeth II
has reigned since 1952,
sent her first e-mail in 1976

Dean Goodluck
Contents

2008/10/18
Netherlands.
Tomatoes and algae
growing in greenhouse

2008/10/19
Value vs Price
Pay 1,500 times more
for bottled water than for tap

2008/10/20
Europe
"Modernity" of centuries-old
convents and monasteries

2008/10/21
"Silicon Forest"
hosting new tech
as many cities do

Four Steps Wiser - WtP Reading & Reflection Vol. 04

Contents

2008/10/22
"I haven't paid for gas in 3 years",
says contestant in
3-day auto race without gasoline

2008/10/23
"Men go back to the mountains,
as they go back to
sailing ships at sea..."
- Henry David Thoreau

2008/10/23
Catching free sunlight:
new vigor of old factory

2008/10/24
Any road for a car
fast enough
to outrun a bullet?

Dean Goodluck
Contents

2008/10/25
5,400 metric tons
of the gas in the atmosphere,
11% tonnage increase per year

2008/10/26
Nature's beauty
on island

2008/10/27
New Zealand Herald:
supermarket food prices
skyrocketing

2008/10/27
"Every doctor
will allow a colleague
to decimate a whole countryside
sooner than..."
- Bernard Shaw

Four Steps Wiser - WtP Reading & Reflection Vol. 04

Contents

2008/10/28
Perth
340,000 spectators
at Air Race World Championship

2008/10/29
Poem
"That all they ask
is rougher weather,
And dory and master
will sail
by fate
To seek the Happy Isles together"
- Robert Frost

2008/10/30
Mobile Library
Librarian does so much
with so little

Dean Goodluck
Contents

2008/10/31
Photography Prize
Prix Pictet

2008/11/01
Who doesn't love chocolate?
Catch the show!

2008/11/02
What happened to Boston-based
general-interest paper,
7-Pulitzer-prize winner?

2008/11/03
Last flew in 1990: 2,300 miles
in 1 hour 4 minutes 20 seconds

2008/11/04
2008 hopes for change
fewer wars, less debt

Four Steps Wiser - WcP Reading & Reflection Vol. 04

Contents

2008/11/05
A major discovery
in the Patagonian rainforest

2008/11/06
Festival of Lights

2008/11/07
Sculptures on cliffs or at shore
attract 500,000 sightseers

2008/11/07
In the middle of Rhine,
Charles III of France
and Henry I of Germany
signed a treaty

2008/11/08
A cosmic figure
hard to figure out

Dean Goodluck

Contents

2008/11/09
They must be true
to their beliefs

2008/11/10
Creatively use
space in and around home

2008/11/11
Laid first wreath
– no one alive has attended
ceremony for the fallen
more times than the Queen

2008/11/12
Visiting Berlin

2008/11/13
Vow of a young king
a nation high in the Himalayas

Four Steps Wiser - WtP Reading & Reflection Vol. 04

Contents

2008/11/14
Poem in Art
"Of Time long past:
And, was it sadness or delight..."
- Percy Bysshe Shelley

2008/11/15
Nothing wasted in Nature
ocean wave farm

2008/11/16
Go Solo
sailing adventure and race

2008/11/17
Car now has wings to fly

2008/11/18
Europe
More bikes, more fun

Dean Goodluck

Contents

2008/11/19
BRIC nations at the
global Financial Stability Forum

2008/11/20
Entire 15-nation euro zone
all declare recession

2008/11/21
Mickey Mouse,
never short of humour

2008/11/22
Spain. Navarra:
70% of electricity
from wind and solar

2008/11/23
Nature's Gold
- LuCxeed Photography

Four Steps Wiser - WtP Reading & Reflection Vol. 04

Contents

2008/11/24
Brazil
When a city is determined
to fight visual pollution

2008/11/25
Tiny Satellite on most powerful
natural particle accelerator

2008/11/26
"Nothing discernible
to the eye of the spirit
is more brilliant or obscure
than man..."
- Victor Hugo

2008/11/27
World's largest island
in midwinter darkness
casts vote

Dean Goodluck

Contents

2008/11/28
Reasonable doubt

2008/11/29
Somalia: troubled waters

2008/11/30
Wisdom with Photo Art
"Before God we are all equally wise
- and equally foolish."
- Albert Einstein

2008/12/01
Fall of housing prices
rise in mortgage foreclosures

2008/12/02
Cartoon
"Prevent another disaster?
Bail me out!"

Four Steps Wiser - WcP Reading & Reflection Vol. 04
Contents

2008/12/03
Venice
Underwater dam
to protect the city

2008/12/04
German troops to France

2008/12/05
Photos
nature's everyday wonders

2008/12/06
Ignorance is Bliss.
"Market Correction
- the day after you buy stocks";
"Standard and Poor
- your life in a nutshell";
"Broker - what my broker
has made me"

Dean Goodluck

Contents

2008/12/07
Indonesia
First Asian Beach Games
opening ceremony

2008/12/08
Promise promised in speech

2008/12/09
Wake Up
- LuCxeed Photography

2008/12/10
"Land of Cheese"
old technologies dominate

2008/12/10
France. 1799:
first uniformity
of weights and measures

Four Steps Wiser - WtP Reading & Reflection Vol. 04

Contents

2008/12/10
Ada Lovelace, a star born

2008/12/11
Nobel Prize split

2008/12/12
Bailout logic?
Listen to Ted Turner

2008/12/13
Lyrical Poem
"Soldier's Engagement Ring"

2008/12/14
"It was darkness
which produced the lamp.
It was fog
that produced the compass."
- Victor Hugo

Dean Goodluck
Contents

2008/12/15
Fleet of 170
emission zero

2008/12/16
Orbital inclination: 51.64 degrees
Orbital speed: 7.67 km/s
Orbital period: 92.49 minutes
Orbits per day: 15.54

2008/12/17
Movie Critic
father's humour
rescues daughter

2008/12/18
Cartoons
amazing variety
arriving at hearing;
newlyweds and runaway car

Four Steps Wiser - WeP Reading & Reflection Vol. 04

Contents

2008/12/19
Beauty and Quality
Zurich, Vienna, Vancouver,
Auckland, Munich, Sydney...

2008/12/20
His serial number: 53310761
his income cut from $400,000
to $78 a month

2008/12/21
Into Shape
- LuCxeed Photography

2008/12/22
Chico
Standing forest

2008/12/23
Bottom line

Dean Goodluck

Contents

2008/12/24
In the season of Joy

2008/12/25
1659 - 1681
Christmas outlawed

2008/12/26
Think Ahead
"To a Greener Earth"

2008/12/26
ThinkAhead™ Calendar
vision in visuals

2008/12/27
"Intellectuals solve problems;
geniuses prevent them."
- Albert Einstein

Four Steps Wiser - WcP Reading & Reflection Vol. 04

Contents

2008/12/28
2,600 BC:
2,300,000 2.5-ton blocks of stone

2008/12/29
"For Kids
the Future of Our World"

2008/12/30
"Love speaks for Romance,
Love speaks
more for Compassion."
- LuCxeed

2008/12/31
39 countries
on all 7 continents
dance with Matt

Dean Goodluck
Contents

Section 2

Grape holds Wine,
Poetry Philosophy.
~ Leisure reading
along the Journey of
Publishing this Book

Poem in Art
Jealousy
- Sappho

Poem
A Strange Wild Song
- Lewis Carroll

Poem in Art:
The Arctic Lover
- William Cullen Bryant

Four Steps Wiser - WcP Reading & Reflection Vol. 04

Contents

Poem
The Arrow And The Song
- Henry Wadsworth Longfellow

Poem
Paradise Lost: Book 01
(lines 544-654)
- John Milton

Poem
Speech: "Friends, Romans,
countrymen, lend me your ears"
- William Shakespeare

❈ ❈ ❈

World Culture Pictorial®
WcP Blog
Book Covers of Other Volumes
in the Series

Dean Goodluck

www.worldculturepictorial.com/blog/archive/all/2008/10/12

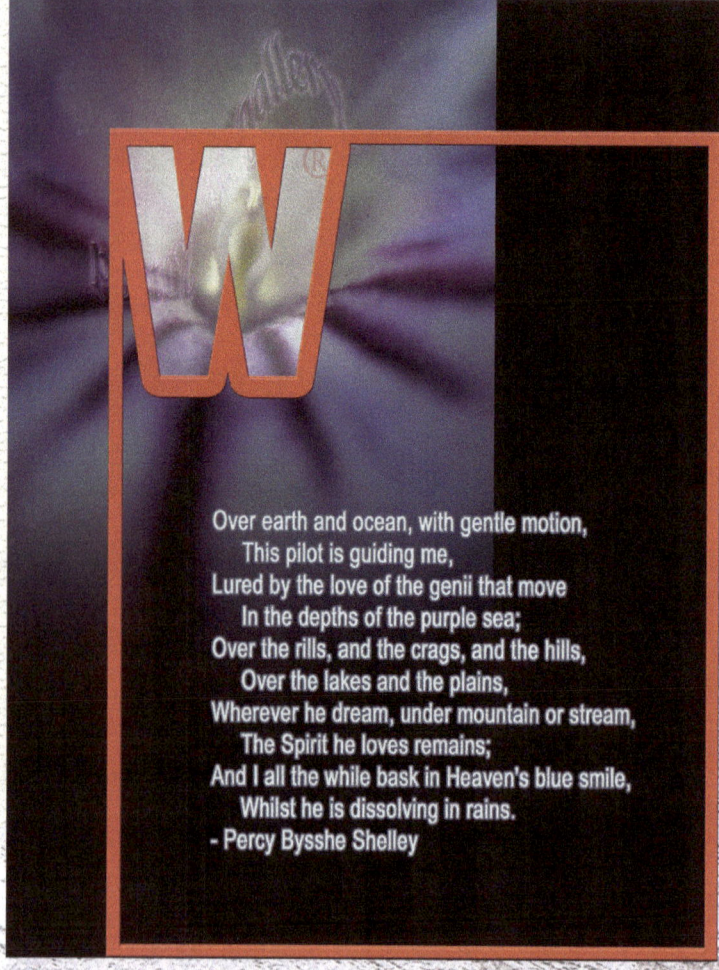

Over earth and ocean, with gentle motion,
   This pilot is guiding me,
Lured by the love of the genii that move
   In the depths of the purple sea;
Over the rills, and the crags, and the hills,
   Over the lakes and the plains,
Wherever he dream, under mountain or stream,
   The Spirit he loves remains;
And I all the while bask in Heaven's blue smile,
   Whilst he is dissolving in rains.
- Percy Bysshe Shelley

Four Steps Wiser - WcP Reading & Reflection Vol. 04

2008/10/12
WcP.Poetic.Thought

Poem in Art
"Over Earth and Ocean,
with gentle motion..."
Percy Bysshe Shelley

Over Earth and Ocean,
　　with gentle motion,
This pilot is guiding me,
Lured by the love of the genii that move
In the depths of the purple sea;
Over the rills, and the crags, and the hills,
Over the lakes and the plains,
Wherever he dream,
　　under mountain or stream,
The Spirit he loves remains;
And I all the while bask
　　in Heaven's blue smile,
Whilst he is dissolving in rains.

- from The Cloud by Percy Bysshe Shelley

Dean Goodluck

Reader Comments

(not in chronological order)
- 2016/05/24 – "I've cried after reading this poem. This poem is a unique example of lightness and very tender feeling. I've saved this poem and gonna show it this evening to my friends. They love different writing techniques but this one is totally generous!"
- 2017/04/21 – "I love to read these short poems. Some are really wonderful in the way they have written and presented before the readers. It must be mentioned that the poet has done a great job and it seems to be a nice one for the readers."
- 2017/02/08 – "Am actually amazed that you can attain such level of sophistication today."

Four Steps Wiser - WeP Reading & Reflection Vol. 04

- 2015/11/29 - "This poem has brought a new light in every reader. It was so clam and subtle which can really bring the most amazing feeling."
- 2015/11/25 - "Over the earth and ocean is a beautiful poem so far I have read and such a simple and subtle one. I wonder how people get those ideas."
- 2016/04/17 - "Very nice to read these lines! I liked this poem very much. I think it conveys something interesting in a simple way. I am so glad to get this opportunity. Thank you so much for sharing this post here. Keep updating!"

Dean Goodluck

2008/10/13
WCP.System.Thinker

Tech vs Ocean
Fishing machines fast
fishing nets vast

Senseless overfishing - world's marine fisheries losing $50 billion each year

www.worldculturepictorial.com/blog/archive/all/2008/10/13

Four Steps Wiser - WcP Reading & Reflection Vol. 04

2008/10/14
WcP.Scientific.Mind

Sun unusually quiet no observed sunspots in 200 days

The Sun is now super quiet, solar wind also dropped to lowest levels in 50 years. Scientists are unsure of the significance of this unusual calm

www.worldculturepictorial.com/blog/archive/all/2008/10/14

Reader Comments

- 2017/10/13 - "All of these pictures are extra efficient and it can only happen in NASA from Academy of Sciences. I am a researcher and I salute to all the researchers who did the flawless job to find cool dense plasma."

Dean Goodluck

2008/10/15
WCP.System.Thinker

unpleasant
25% of North Pole Arctic
naked without ice

At top of Earth, Arctic ice shrunk by 25%, left islandlike ice cap surrounded by open water, 181 Alaskan villages face erosion

www.worldculturepictorial.com/blog/archive/all/2008/10/15

Four Steps Wiser - WcP Reading & Reflection Vol. 04

2008/10/16
WcP.Scientific.Mind

I was like a boy playing on the sea-shore...

"I was like a boy playing on the sea-shore,
and diverting myself now and then
finding a smoother pebble
or a prettier shell than ordinary,
whilst the great ocean of truth
lay all undiscovered before me."
- Isaac Newton

www.worldculturepictorial.com/blog/archive/all/2008/10/16

Dean Goodluck

2008/10/17
WCP.Humor

Queen Elizabeth II has reigned since 1952, sent her first e-mail in 1976

Royal giggles and Google Doodle - Queen Elizabeth II visits Google's UK headquarters, views laughing baby video

www.worldculturepictorial.com/ blog/ archive/ all/ 2008/ 10/ 17

(not in chronological order)
- 2012/06/12 – "It is wonderful that the royal house is trying to keep in contact with the new technologies and be modern. I would like USA to be a monarchy so that we could have the same values and respect as the British citizens."
- 2010/09/21 – "awesome article"
- 2013/09/16 – "lovely article"

Four Steps Wiser - WcP Reading & Reflection Vol. 04

2008/10/18
WcP.Observer

Netherlands.
Tomatoes and algae
growing in greenhouse

Jet plane to fly on algae-based fuel by 2010? Europe's algae bloom aims for feasible alternative to fossil fuel

www.worldculturepictorial.com/blog/archive/all/2008/10/18

Dean Goodluck

2008/10/19
WCP.Life.Coach

Value vs Price
Pay 1,500 times more for bottled water than for tap

Convenience at a cost. Bottled water no less polluted than kitchen tap, in addition to plastic pollution

www.worldculturepictorial.com/blog/archive/all/2008/10/19

Four Steps Wiser - WcP Reading & Reflection Vol. 04

2008/10/20
WcP.Story.Teller

Europe
"Modernity" of centuries-old convents and monasteries

Monks and nuns become hoteliers in economically challenging times: monastic doors open for travelers in Europe

www.worldculturepictorial.com/blog/archive/all/2008/10/20

Reader Comments

- 2008/10/19 - "This article is great as it lists lots of places to stay. I'm planning a trip to Italy and I found the same website about convents. They have places all over Italy and look to be very reasonably priced."

Dean Goodluck

2008/10/21
WCP.Market.Watch

"Silicon Forest"
hosting new tech
as many cities do

Techies' new frontiers: Portland OR, Bethlehem PA, Blacksburg VA, Bellevue WA, Boise ID, Folsom CA

www.worldculturepictorial.com/blog/archive/all/2008/10/21

Reader Comments

- 2016/04/01 – "Well Admin! I have gotten impressed awfully due to this article which no doubt keep conferring me tremendous information. Thanks for writing on it."
- 2016/04/12 – "Great writing it is such a good and nice idea thanks for sharing your article. I like your post. Thanks…"

Four Steps Wiser - WcP Reading & Reflection Vol. 04

2008/10/22
wcP.Scientific.Mind

"I haven't paid for gas in 3 years", says contestant in 3-day auto race without gasoline

Inventors in 800mi car race run on wood chips, cow dung, veg oil, no gas! Jagged Sierra Nevada, bleak flatness of Death Valley

www.worldculturepictorial.com/blog/archive/all/2008/10/22

Reader Comments

♦ 2012/08/21 - "I am so amazed by this cute, small lime-green pickup truck that is canola oil powered. I like the idea of the competition having vehicles run by vegetable oil, alcohol etc. Congrats to the winners. I'd love to ride in one of those creations."

Dean Goodluck

2008/10/23
wcp.life.Coach

Men go back to the mountains,
as they go back to
sailing ships at sea...

"Men go back to the mountains, as they go back to sailing ships at sea, because in the mountains and on the sea they must face up."
- Henry David Thoreau

www.worldculturepictorial.com/blog/archive/all/2008/10/23

Four Steps Wiser - WcP Reading & Reflection Vol. 04

2008/10/23
WcP.Observer

*Catching free sunlight:
new vigor of old factory*

Genius. Recycled silicon wafer factory, flipped switch on US' largest solar cell plant: German SolarWorld AG

www.worldculturepictorial.com/blog/archive/all/2008/10/23

Dean Goodluck

2008/10/24
WCP.Scientific.Mind

Any road for a car fast enough to outrun a bullet?

Faster than a speeding bullet - world's first 1000-mph supersonic car "Bloodhound" to be built by British engineers

www.worldculturepictorial.com/blog/archive/all/2008/10/24

Reader Comments

♦ 2015/02/13 - "I constantly spend my half an hour to read this website's articles everyday along with a cup of coffee."

Four Steps Wiser - WcP Reading & Reflection Vol. 04

2008/10/25
WcP.Watchful.Eye

5,400 metric tons of the gas in the atmosphere, 11% tonnage increase per year

A greenhouse gas 17000 times more potent than CO2: NF3 gas used in making flat panel TVs, computer displays, microcircuits

www.worldculturepictorial.com/blog/archive/all/2008/10/25

Reader Comments

- 2016/10/22 - "The result of the study is alarming and an eye opener to hazards of climate change induced as a result of greenhouse gases. Surely the information technology sector needs to come up with an alternative way of manufacturing which is sustainable so that the amounts of emissions produced are less."
- 2016/10/13 - "I would really like to thank for your article it's really helpful. Regards."

Dean Goodluck

2008/10/26
WCP.Story.Teller

Nature's beauty on island

Kangaroo Island, Australia's Galapagos, zoo without fences: kangaroos, wallabies, bandicoots, koalas, and 5-star service

www.worldculturepictorial.com/blog/archive/all/2008/10/26

Reader Comments

◆ 2016/05/07 – "This amazing country must be one of the most beautiful in the world."

Four Steps Wiser - WcP Reading & Reflection Vol. 04

2008/10/27
WcP.System.Thinker

New Zealand Herald: supermarket food prices skyrocketing

Bailout: Decrease financial digits in stock market? Or decrease quantity of food with increasing prices?

www.worldculturepictorial.com/blog/archive/all/2008/10/27

Dean Goodluck

2008/10/27
WCP.Humor

Every doctor will allow a colleague to decimate a whole countryside sooner than...

"Every doctor will allow a colleague to decimate a whole countryside sooner than violate the bond of professional etiquette by giving him away."
- Bernard Shaw

www.worldculturepictorial.com/blog/archive/all/2008/10/27

Four Steps Wiser - WcP Reading & Reflection Vol. 04

2008/10/28
WcP.Observer

Perth
340,000 spectators
at Air Race World Championship

Red Bull Air Race - pilots fly aerobatic planes (top speeds > 250mph/400 kph) through series of gates, perform specific maneuvers

www.worldculturepictorial.com/blog/archive/all/2008/10/28

Dean Goodluck

2008/10/29
WCP.Poetic.Thought

Poem
"That all they ask is rougher weather,
And dory and master will sail by fate
To seek the Happy Isles together"
Robert Frost

The fisherman's swapping a yarn for a yarn
Under the hand of the village barber,
And her in the angle of house and barn
His deep-sea dory has found a harbor.

At anchor she rides the sunny sod
As full to the gunnel of flowers growing
As ever she turned her home with cod
From George's bank
    when winds were blowing.

And I judge from that elysian freight
That all they ask is rougher weather,
And dory and master will sail by fate
To seek the Happy Isles together.

- The Flower Boat by Robert Frost

www.worldculturepictorial.com/blog/archive/all/2008/10/29

Four Steps Wiser - WcP Reading & Reflection Vol. 04

2008/10/30
WcP.Story.Teller

Mobile Library
Librarian does so much
with so little

On 2 donkeys: Columbian library "Biblioburro" with 4800 books - schoolteacher Luis Soriano brings books to villagers

www.worldculturepictorial.com/blog/archive/all/2008/10/30

Reader Comments

(not in chronological order)
♦ 2017/05/10 - "Good to know - I would like to appreciate this man who is really working hard to bring some innovation in education and making children able to learn the best things."

- 2017/07/18 - "How many years have you been a school teacher? I'm 27 and this is now my 5th year. I got my teaching licence when I was 21. I've spent my first three years of teaching in the Philippines and now I am in Japan, still teaching. I love everything about teaching! I couldn't think of me being in a different field."
- 2017/08/03 - "Appreciation - Very good initiative by the Columbian library. This will help us to make education for society. And many good wishes to the teachers who accompany the management in this regard."
- 2017/03/13 - "Nice Post, keep sharing like this."
- 2017/03/10 - "Great post. The school teacher giving education to villagers is great work."
- 2017/03/13 - "Agreed. Admiring the time and effort you put into your blog and detailed information you offer!"
- 2017/03/13 - "This is very nice article according to my judgment. I'm truly inspired with this story."
- 2017/07/18 - "The picture and the post you shared is nice dear."

- 2017/06/13 – "Inspiring Post – It's inspiring and very motivational for students."
- 2017/05/22 – "Good to know about that. I believe that education is the only thing that creates a sense in human being about right and wrong."

Dean Goodluck

2008/10/31
WCP.Art

Photography Prize
Prix Pictet

First international photography prize Prix Pictet: camera to communicate vital dispatch on most serious issues facing us all

www.worldculturepictorial.com/blog/archive/all/2008/10/31

Reader Comments

♦ 2010/11/14 - "You can find a post on the 2010 pictet exhibition in Paris at the gallery Les filles du calvaire at the following address."

Four Steps Wiser - WcP Reading & Reflection Vol. 04

2008/11/01
WcP.Art

Who doesn't love chocolate?
Catch the show!

Irresistible! 14th Chocolate Show opens in Paris with 400 exhibitors and 140 chocolatiers from around the world

www.worldculturepictorial.com/blog/archive/all/2008/11/01

Dean Goodluck

2008/11/02
WCP.Tomorrows.History

*What happened to
Boston-based general-interest paper,
7-Pulitzer-prize winner?*

Newspapers' future: news-paperless, or newspaper-less? Century-old Christian Science Monitor ends daily print, goes online

www.worldculturepictorial.com/blog/archive/all/2008/11/02

Four Steps Wiser - WcP Reading & Reflection Vol. 04

2008/11/03
WcP.Scientific.Mind

*Last flew in 1990:
2,300 miles
in 1 hour 4 minutes 20 seconds*

Aircraft and spacecraft once swiftest or slowest, graceful or ungainly, at standstill as if plucked from sky: Air and Space Museum

www.worldculturepictorial.com/blog/archive/all/2008/11/03

Dean Goodluck

2008/11/04
WcP.Observer

*2008 hopes for change
fewer wars, less debt*

2008 election for change - leading US out of debt, world out of war? Obama, Biden won: "two wars, worst financial crisis"

www.worldculturepictorial.com/blog/archive/all/2008/11/04

Four Steps Wiser - WcP Reading & Reflection Vol. 04

2008/11/05
wcP.Scientific.Mind

A major discovery in the Patagonian rainforest

Nature provides. A tree fungus could provide green fuel that can be pumped directly into vehicle tanks: Patagonian rainforest

www.worldculturepictorial.com/blog/archive/all/2008/11/05

Dean Goodluck

2008/11/06
WCP.Story.Teller

Festival of Lights

Diwali, path/array of lights.
Festival of Lights, victory of good over evil, celebrated to dispel darkness and light up lives

www.worldculturepictorial.com/blog/archive/all/2008/11/06

Reader Comments

- 2016/11/30 – "Diwali is the most loving and admirable festival in India celebrated by every individual with no religious or caste differences. And kids really enjoy firing the crackers, every house is filled with beautiful lamps and lighting of firecrackers."
- 2017/01/22 – "Your explanation is so simple yet I can get what Diwali is all about. thank you."
- 2017/02/13 – "wow very nice posting"

Four Steps Wiser - WcP Reading & Reflection Vol. 04

2008/11/07
WcP.Art

Sculptures on cliffs or at shore attract 500,000 sightseers

Sculptures by the Sea - 107 sculptures from 7 countries on display at Australia's largest annual outdoor free exhibition

www.worldculturepictorial.com/blog/archive/all/2008/11/07

Reader Comments

(not in chronological order)
◆ 2016/06/16 – "Sculptures are always very attractive and if it is in beach side it is awesome. I think such exhibition must be conducted every year so that people can watch things and know about the same. Anyway thank you for sharing this article and keep sharing."

- 2016/05/16 - "What a beautiful sculpture it was, never seen it before and just loved the way they are made. There is no end to creativity as i look at them. That was a very good collection from far seven countries."
- 2016/04/25 - "I am interested in understanding more about the different cultures across the world and this site has been helping me by offering awesome posts on culture. Keep up the good work guys. Thank you for sharing the details."
- 2015/08/26 - "I think this art by the beach initiative is a great idea to offer beach-goers something more apart from the breath-taking sunsets and stunning views. We have such displays here in Gold Coast and they attract not only tourists but locals as well. It gives a different experience for people of all ages to enjoy."
- 2016/04/10 - "I am interested in knowing about world history and this site has helped me a lot. The posts that are shared here on the site about world history are very interesting and informative. Keep on sharing more and more posts."

Four Steps Wiser - WcP Reading & Reflection Vol. 04

2008/11/07
WcP.Ambassador

*In the middle of Rhine,
Charles III of France and
Henry I of Germany signed a treaty*

7 Nov 921 Treaty of Bonn: East France and West France recognize each other in a "pact of friendship"

www.worldculturepictorial.com/blog/archive/all/2008/11/07

Dean Goodluck

2008/11/08
WCP.WatchfulEye

*A cosmic figure
hard to figure out*

US national debt: $10+ trillion, increasing $3.99 billion daily. US population: 305 million; each citizen's share: $35k

www.worldculturepictorial.com/blog/archive/all/2008/11/08

Four Steps Wiser - WcP Reading & Reflection Vol. 04

2008/11/09
WcP.Observer

They must be true to their beliefs

Takes courage to be 3rd party candidate - 1860: Abraham Lincoln elected; 1992: Ross Perot; 2008: Bob Barr and Ralph Nader

www.worldculturepictorial.com/blog/archive/all/2008/11/09

Dean Goodluck

2008/11/10
WCP.Scientific.Mind

*Creatively use space
in and around home*

Work of art: house with natural light. Intensely green: sunflower husk wall panels, solar heating, recycled water for garden

www.worldculturepictorial.com/blog/archive/all/2008/11/10

Four Steps Wiser - WcP Reading & Reflection Vol. 04

2008/11/11
WcP.Observer

*Laid first wreath -
no one alive has attended
ceremony for the fallen
more times than the Queen*

Oldest WWI survivors join commemorations on Remembrance Day, pay tribute to fallen millions in 1st, 2nd World Wars

www.worldculturepictorial.com/blog/archive/all/2008/11/11

Reader Comments

- 2015/07/18 - "Great post."
- 2015/08/16 - "I relish, discovered exactly what I was looking for. You have ended my four day long hunt! God Bless you man. Have a nice day."
- 2015/08/16 - "I enjoy the info you present here and can't wait to take a look when I get home. Anyways, awesome site!"
- 2015/10/06 - "This text is priceless. How can I find out more?"

Dean Goodluck

2008/11/12
WCP.Story.Teller

Visiting Berlin

Travel: Berlin in Pictures. Potsdamer Platz, Bode Museum(Kaiser-Friedrich-Museum), Reichstag iconic glass dome, Brandenburg Gate

www.worldculturepictorial.com/blog/archive/all/2008/11/12

Reader Comments

(not in chronological order)

♦ 2010/10/18 - "Schloss charlottenburg is an amazing palace, I think this is the only palace which has not been destroyed during the war, I have been impressed by its rooms which is as it is as they were earlier, the view of the lake bordering Berlin river and the garden is really worth seeing."

Four Steps Wiser - WP Reading & Reflection Vol. 04

- 2011/07/08 - "All the places in Berlin seems to be worth visiting but, i like Potsdamer Platz the most."
- 2012/01/27 - "Berlin is the most beautiful tourist destination. It's really a great place to visit. The Bode Museum is the center of attraction of Berlin. It looks really very stunning. Last month I was in Sydney and I visited Powerhouse Museum. I really love this museum."
- 2016/04/27 - "Crown of Europe. This country has very rich cultural heritage."
- 2016/06/04 - "What a beautiful place is Berlin - by reading this article I am very much excited to plan a trip to Berlin sooner. I am so glad for the best places listed here in Berlin. Being a traveler I really love to go over there. Hope for the best in my trip."
- 2017/03/31 - "Controversial Berlin - When I was in Berlin for the first time, I had a double feeling: how beautiful Berlin is and how dirty it is..."
- 2016/09/15 - "Berlin is pretty - Germany is my favorite place..."
- 2014/05/16 - "Thank you for this knowledge. If only all bloggers open the same level of content as you, the internet would be a much better place."

- 2012/07/13 - "I really liked your article on Berlin. As if I was there. So would like to visit Berlin. I've never been there. But it would take a large sum of money..."
- 2012/07/11 - "The pictures convinced me. I must go to Berlin next holiday. I love travelling and visiting many places. Last time I was in India. If someone goes there I think that visiting Taj Mahal is one of the 7 Things to do on vacation in India."
- 2012/04/30 - "This is so amazing place, maybe this is very expensive place."
- 2012/02/09 - "Everything is very open and very clear explanation of issues. Your website is very useful. Thanks for sharing."
- 2017/03/23 - "Such a great post very powerful post with travel."
- 2012/05/21 - "Yes what can we say about this culture pictorial but one can say that information is perfect indeed."

Four Steps Wiser - WcP Reading & Reflection Vol. 04

2008/11/13
WcP.Observer

Vow of a young king a nation high in the Himalayas

"Maintain the Gross National Happiness", vows 28-year old Oxford graduate newly crowned the fifth King of Bhutan

www.worldculturepictorial.com/blog/archive/all/2008/11/13

Dean Goodluck

www.worldculturepictorial.com/blog/archive/all/2008/11/14

Like the ghost of a dear friend dead
Is Time long past.
A tone which is now forever fled,
A hope which is now forever past,
A love so sweet it could not last,
Was Time long past.

There were sweet dreams in the night
Of Time long past:
And, was it sadness or delight,
Each day a shadow onward cast
Which made us wish it yet might last—
That Time long past.

   - Percy Bysshe Shelley

Four Steps Wiser - WcP Reading & Reflection Vol. 04

2008/11/14
WcP.Poetic.Thought

Poem in Art
"Of Time long past:
And, was it sadness or delight..."
Percy Bysshe Shelley

Like the ghost of a dear friend dead
Is Time long past.
A tone which is now forever fled,
A hope which is now forever past,
A love so sweet it could not last,
Was Time long past.

There were sweet dreams in the night
Of Time long past:
And, was it sadness or delight,
Each day a shadow onward cast
Which made us wish it yet might last -
That Time long past.

- from Time Long Past
by Percy Bysshe Shelley

Dean Goodluck

2008/11/15
WCP.Scientific.Mind

*Nothing wasted in Nature
ocean wave farm*

World first. Ever-restless ocean wave farm generates electricity for 1,500 homes on shore: Pelamis in Portugal

www.worldculturepictorial.com/blog/archive/all/2008/11/15

Reader Comments

♦ 2008/11/16 - *"The earth itself provides so many ways to capture energy, from wind to sun to tides. The forces of nature, based on gravity and attraction of celestial objects, are waiting for us to harness. Much more respectful of the planet than burning fuel."*

Four Steps Wiser - WcP Reading & Reflection Vol. 04

- 2011/10/10 - "This is an interesting technology indeed. The current version of this technology is not yet at its most efficient, but I am sure science as it ways to make it so. However, if Portugal decides to fully rely on this wave energy, wouldn't it deface the beautiful seas with those machines?"
- 2012/03/13 - "One of the fears I have is that if such a technology is refined and becomes massively popular, more and more countries living close to the sea will start to implement this wave farm to generate their electrical energy. Will we see our shores filled with these wave farms? Would this affect the marine life in anyway?"
- 2013/08/21 - "This is very much interesting. Thanks for sharing this useful information."

Dean Goodluck

2008/11/16
WCP.Story.Teller

Go Solo
sailing adventure and race

Vendée Globe yacht race: 23k-mile round-the-world alone, non-stop no-assist, via South Pole and back in 60ft monohulls

www.worldculturepictorial.com/ blog/ archive/ all/ 2008/11/16

Reader Comments

- 2008/11/16 - "If you fancy following the Vendee in a bit more detail I'm writing a blog. Jonny's the 34 year old skipper of another British boat called Artemis. I'm his brother and his friends and family are working together to cover the 26,000 mile race using only a blog and Twitter. Jonny is 'tweeting' from the boat as he goes (as far as we know this is a first) and they go directly onto the blog. Come and let us know what you think. It's all a bit of an experiment but it's fun. We're using free media to see if we can do something different and a bit more organic than the 'official' race sites (which all look ridiculously expensive but lack a sense of community)."

Dean Goodluck

2008/11/17
WCP.Scientific.Mind

Car now has wings to fly

World's first biofuel-powered flying car - Parajet Skycar drives like a car and flies like a plane

www.worldculturepictorial.com/blog/archive/all/2008/11/17

Reader Comments

- 2012/07/05 – "Wow! This is a brilliant idea! I recently made a car donation towards a group that makes this kind of projects. I really hope they can stabilize such a car and even mass produce them. I would love to ride one of these skycars in the near future."
- "2013/03/25 – The car looks interesting and due to bio fuel it is safe also. Should carry on inventing and bettering automobiles like this."

Four Steps Wiser - WcP Reading & Reflection Vol. 04

- 2012/07/31 - "Electric Cars emit no tailpipe pollutants, although the power plant producing the electricity may emit them. Electricity from nuclear-, hydro-, solar-, or wind-powered plants causes no air pollutants. Electric motors provide quiet, smooth operation and stronger acceleration and require less maintenance than ICEs."
- 2012/08/03 - "This is so amazing! With the traffic problems and parking scarcity we experienced on land, this seems to be a great idea. It must have been very expensive building this kind. This might be made from branded and quality car parts which maybe lighter. Makes me wonder about its differences with the usual cars. Are flying cars now the future of driving? I'd love to ride on one of this someday, hopefully. :)"
- 2012/10/18 - "Now can you imagine the traffic in the air?? I believe we'll face it in near 50 years.. This car is good to cross rivers by air to looking for the nearest bridge))"
- 2017/05/01 - "Since years people are anticipating for such flying cars as they are so cool and there is no limit of speed and issue of traffic if it's driven in the sky."
- 2017/09/18 - "Hey there, i think this is wonderful. Imagine all those traffic troubles just gone. No more waiting, only freedom! Flying cars wow!"

Dean Goodluck

2008/11/18
WCP.Observer

Europe
More bikes, more fun

Europe loves bikes. Assembly lines of biggest facility in Europe have average output of 3000 bikes per day, 1 million in 2009

www.worldculturepictorial.com/blog/archive/all/2008/11/18

Reader Comments

♦ 2012/04/23 - "Europe is known as one of the biggest markets for bikes. European countries are big lovers of bikes. I think at this stage the output is more than 5000 units per day."

Four Steps Wiser - WcP Reading & Reflection Vol. 04

2008/11/19
WcP.Market.Watch

BRIC nations at the global Financial Stability Forum

Global financial summit from G7 to G20; new strong voice of BRIC nations: Brazil, Russia, India and China

www.worldculturepictorial.com/blog/archive/all/2008/11/19

Reader Comments

(not in chronological order)
♦ 2016/05/31 – "Financial crisis is a word I am hearing every day and I think we are facing many problems due to this. This is a good way to inform people about developing countries and their financial details and thank you for sharing the info."

- ♦ 2008/11/20 - "Shift in Global Power is in Process - This move to expand the sphere of influence with regards to making global policy decisions in long overdue and illustrates the fact that emerging nations must have a voice at the table. This will not only affect the financial markets, but will include those issues related to the environment and climate change. It will be important for the US and Europe to facilitate this shift rather than pushing back, as has been the approach to date."
- ♦ 2016/05/25 - "I don't know much about financial crisis and the things associated with it. But I am happy to hear about the decisions made by the national leaders to fight against this crisis. Thank you for sharing valuable and informative articles like this."
- ♦ 2016/05/20 - "This is good news that developing countries are also getting an opportunity to participate in financial summits. These summits were only organized by developed nations and their finical issues only. But, G7 Has now became G20 including developing nations which have strong financial status. BRIC is formed by these four nations they provide financial help to the needed nation."

Four Steps Wiser - WcP Reading & Reflection Vol. 04

- 2016/04/27 - "The blog always shares some great news articles and I really like to read news from here. The pictures and articles shared in this post are also every informative and I would like to take this moment to thank the precious one who posts such interesting news."
- 2016/04/12 - "The news and articles like this are read by everyone but it is from this site I have come to know more about the same news. You people have perfectly written about the particular news and the main attractions of the news and thanks for sharing the news."
- 2013/11/06 - "It's good to hear that the national leaders decided to get involved in the fight to combat financial crisis. I am sure their assistants know the basics and can give them valuable ideas on how to implement different strategies that would stop the spread to the developing economies."

Dean Goodluck

2008/11/20
WCP.Story.Teller

Entire 15-nation euro zone all declare recession

Buffett said in March, US in recession; now, recession declared by Germany, Italy, 15 Eurozone nations, and Japan

www.worldculturepictorial.com/blog/archive/all/2008/11/20

Reader Comments

♦ 2015/08/03 – "The housing program is even affected by this recession despite being put as one of their priorities of changes. Sadly, nothing seems been started and done due to the cases that make the economy freeze."

Four Steps Wiser - WcP Reading & Reflection Vol. 04

2008/11/21
WcP.Humor

Mickey Mouse, never short of humour

Mickey Mouse turns 80 - symbol of optimism, fun, zest for life, raised a smile from almost everyone he has touched

www.worldculturepictorial.com/blog/archive/all/2008/11/21

Reader Comments

- 2014/04/22 - "Hats off to Elias Disney!! We all know that Mickey Mouse is undoubtedly the most famous cartoon character in the world. Elias Disney was obviously a highly talented and creative artist. He is one of the best artists the world has ever seen. No one else could have imagined a mouse with this cool and amusing appearance. Hats off to him!!"
- 2012/05/03 - "Thanks to this trivia, this is how Mickey evolved."

Dean Goodluck

2008/11/22
WCP.Scientific.Mind

Spain. Navarra: 70% of electricity from wind and solar

Solar Energy: Spain 4th in world, 2nd in Europe behind Germany; number of solar companies leapt from a couple dozen to a few hundred

www.worldculturepictorial.com/blog/archive/all/2008/11/22

Reader Comments

♦ 2008/11/23 – "Solar Moves Foward – The Mediterranean is one of the ideal areas in the world to take advantage of solar energy and Spain's leadership in this arena will go far to inspire others to follow suit. There are also many opportunities to implement this technology in an artistic way that enhances a structure's physical beauty while reminding us of the movement that is underway."

♦ 2008/11/23 - "It is so good to see Spain taking the initiative as one of the few Mediterranean countries to adopt solar power on a mass scale. I mean the Med has some of the sunniest countries in Europe - for example Cyprus has 332 days of sunshine a year - so it makes sense for them to use solar power.
Just imagine the possibilities if the others followed suit - South-western Europe's power could eventually come from more than 20% renewable energy. This could also lead to mass production and lower unit costs, making solar power even more attractive.
I guess only time will tell..."

Dean Goodluck

2008/11/23
WCP.Art

LuCxeed Photography
Nature's Gold

www.worldculturepictorial.com/blog/archive/all/2008/11/23

Four Steps Wiser - WcP Reading & Reflection Vol. 04

2008/11/24
WcP.Observer

Brazil
When a city is determined
to fight visual pollution

"Clean City" São Paulo says no to visual pollution, 15,000 billboards, 1,600 signs, 1,300 towering metal panels removed

www.worldculturepictorial.com/blog/archive/all/2008/11/24

Reader Comments

- 2016/02/25 - "Large cities are the most affected by pollution and if banning public advertising will make a change for the better, then so be it. Living in a large city might sound tempting, but for a few years now, increasingly more people would rather live in custom homes than in a city center apartment. It has many advantages, but the most important are the improved living standards and the energy efficiency."
- 2016/04/27 - "I've read some just right stuff here. Certainly bookmarking for revisiting. I'm surprised how much effort you set to make the sort of excellent informative site."
- 2017/12/13 - "Superb article and I would really like to thank you for your article it's really helpful. Regards."

Four Steps Wiser - WcP Reading & Reflection Vol. 04

2008/11/25
WcP.Scientific.Mind

*Tiny Satellite
on most powerful
natural particle accelerator*

Bread-loaf-sized satellite Firefly on lightning and gamma rays (photon of penetrating electromagnetic radiation from atomic nucleus)

www.worldculturepictorial.com/blog/archive/all/2008/11/25

Dean Goodluck

2008/11/26
WCP.Philosophy

*Nothing discernible
to the eye of the spirit
is more brilliant or obscure
than man...*

"Nothing discernible
to the eye of the spirit
is more brilliant or obscure than man;
nothing is more formidable, complex,
mysterious, and infinite.
There is a prospect greater than the sea,
and it is the sky;
there is a prospect greater than the sky,
and it is the human soul."
- Victor Hugo

www.worldculturepictorial.com/blog/archive/all/2008/11/26

Four Steps Wiser - WcP Reading & Reflection Vol. 04

2008/11/27
WcP.Observer

*World's largest island
in midwinter darkness
casts vote*

Greenland, semiautonomous Danish territory, takes symbolic leap: 75% voters vote for independence. Oil, key issue?

www.worldculturepictorial.com/blog/archive/all/2008/11/27

Dean Goodluck

2008/11/28
WcP.Observer

Reasonable doubt

Troop increases in Afghanistan; soldiers doubt sense of mission: "Politicians need to clarify it more clearly"

www.worldculturepictorial.com/blog/archive/all/2008/11/28

Four Steps Wiser - WcP Reading & Reflection Vol. 04

2008/11/29
WcP.Story.Teller

Somalia: troubled waters

Piracy renewed: almost 40 ships seized by Somali pirates and more than $150m (£101m) in ransoms paid so far this year

www.worldculturepictorial.com/blog/archive/all/2008/11/29

Dean Goodluck

www.worldculturepictorial.com/blog/archive/all/2008/11/30

Before God we are all equally wise – and equally foolish. Albert Einstein

Window to the Wind of Wisdom

Four Steps Wiser - WcP Reading & Reflection Vol. 04

2008/11/30
WcP.Humor

Wall Decor:
Wisdom with Photo Art
"Before God we are all equally wise - and equally foolish."

"Before God we are all equally wise - and equally foolish."
- Albert Einstein

Reader Comments

♦ 2008/12/01 - "Wise Words to Remember- It's often the case that when we think we're wisest, God is smiling."

Dean Goodluck

2008/12/01
WCP.Market.Watch

*Fall of housing prices
rise in mortgage foreclosures*

Now it's official: US in recession since 2007, one of the longest downturns since the Great Depression of 1930's

www.worldculturepictorial.com/blog/archive/all/2008/12/01

Reader Comments

♦ 2008/12/01 - "No Easy Out This Time - What's hard to predict about this recession is the length and severity, as the conditions present this time around have never occurred before, especially the total collapse of the credit markets and the inability of governments around the globe to fix it."

Four Steps Wiser - WcP Reading & Reflection Vol. 04

2008/12/02
WcP.Common.Sense

Cartoon
"Prevent another disaster?
Bail me out!"

Bailout fever rescue economy or Market correct itself? How many trillions are enough? Who shouldn't be bailed out?

www.worldculturepictorial.com/blog/archive/all/2008/12/02

Dean Goodluck

2008/12/03
WCP.WatchfulEye

*Venice
Underwater dam
to protect the city*

Venice hit by biggest flood in 20 years, waters rising quickly to 1.56m/5ft. Famous St Mark's Square submerged

www.worldculturepictorial.com/ blog/ archive/ all/ 2008/ 12/ 03

Four Steps Wiser - WcP Reading & Reflection Vol. 04

2008/12/04
WcP.Tomorrows.History

German troops to France

History sees sharp turn: 1st time since WWII, German troops to station in France; France to withdraw from Germany

www.worldculturepictorial.com/blog/archive/all/2008/12/04

Dean Goodluck

2008/12/05
WCP.Poetic.Thought

Photos
nature's everyday wonders

Portraits of wondrous Earth: ice storm glazed tree; poetic snowflakes; ice caverns; Giant's Causeway; geysers; sea unicorns

www.worldculturepictorial.com/blog/archive/all/2008/12/05

Reader Comments

- 2008/12/07 – "Amazing Nature – We often take nature for granted and never stop to think about the intricate physics that serves as a foundation for so much natural beauty. These examples are so diverse, it's hard to believe they could come from the same planet."

Four Steps Wiser - WcP Reading & Reflection Vol. 04

2008/12/06
WcP.Humor

Ignorance is Bliss.
"Market Correction - the day after
you buy stocks"; "Standard and Poor
- your life in a nutshell"; "Broker -
what my broker has made me"

Ignorance is Bliss. Value Investing: art of buying low and selling lower... Cartoon: Stock Market Roller Coaster

www.worldculturepictorial.com/blog/archive/all/2008/12/06

Reader Comments

◆ 2017/03/21 – "I hadn't really known about many stock market and business terms but coming over here, I've learned plenty of new things. Thanks for spreading the information, it's allowed me to be much more proactive on my business meetings."

Dean Goodluck

2008/12/07
WCP.Life.Coach

Indonesia
First Asian Beach Games
opening ceremony

Inaugural 2008 Asian Beach Games in Bali, Indonesia promote sports and culture: 6000 athletes, 71 events, 19 sports

www.worldculturepictorial.com/blog/archive/all/2008/12/07

Four Steps Wiser - WcP Reading & Reflection Vol. 04

2008/12/08
WcP.Tomorrows.History

Promise promised in speech

2008's Promise. Obama: "I still think the mission to get out of [Iraq] as soon as possible will be accomplished."

www.worldculturepictorial.com/blog/archive/all/2008/12/08

Reader Comments

♦ 2016/01/13 – "Being a student of politics I always try to study content relevant to my field no matter it's on paper or online. The reason is that I am providing superior papers review to my juniors to let them learn with my knowledge. With my experience I have observed that cabinet was the one in the history of America involved in wars all the time which is not in favor of anyone."

- ♦ 2016/06/09 - "Hi there, I am so grateful I found your website, I really found you by error, while I was looking on AOL for something else. Anyways I am here now and would just like to say many thanks for a fantastic post and an all round interesting blog (I also love the theme/design), I don't have time to read through it all at the moment but I have book-marked it and also added in your RSS feeds, so when I have time I will be back to read a lot more, Please do keep up the awesome blog."
- ♦ 2016/10/27 - "This is a truly good site post. Not too many people would actually, the way you just did. I am really impressed that there is so much information about this subject that has been uncovered and you've done your best, with so much class."
- ♦ 2016/10/27 - "Wonderful blog! I found it while surfing around on Yahoo News."

Four Steps Wiser - WcP Reading & Reflection Vol. 04

2008/12/09
WcP.art

LuCxeed Photography
Wake Up

www.worldculturepictorial.com/blog/archive/all/2008/12/09

Dean Goodluck

2008/12/10
WCP.Story.Teller

"Land of Cheese"
old technologies dominate

"Land of Cheese" Asturias, Spain: thousands of caves hidden in hills used by residents for centuries to age cheese

www.worldculturepictorial.com/blog/archive/all/2008/12/10

Four Steps Wiser - WcP Reading & Reflection Vol. 04

2008/12/10
WcP.Scientific.Mind

*France, 1799:
first uniformity
of weights and measures*

10 Dec 1799: France adopts the metric system, first country to do so

www.worldculturepictorial.com/blog/archive/all/2008/12/10

Dean Goodluck

2008/12/10
WCP.Scientific.Mind

*Ada Lovelace
a star born*

10 Dec 1915: the first computer programmer, daughter of Lord Byron, Ada Lovelace born in London

www.worldculturepictorial.com/blog/archive/all/2008/12/10

Four Steps Wiser - WcP Reading & Reflection Vol. 04

2008/12/11

Nobel Prize split

Where top talents go, so does Nobel Prize. Japan shares chemistry prize, splits physics award with American scientists

www.worldculturepictorial.com/ blog/ archive/ all/ 2008/ 12/ 11

Dean Goodluck

2008/12/12
WCP.Humor

Bailout logic?
Listen to Ted Turner

Bailout logic? Ted Turner: "I've never asked for a bailout. Where does it end?"
Big Three asks for $25 billion

www.worldculturepictorial.com/blog/archive/all/2008/12/12

Reader Comments

♦ "Hi, hope the bailout is not the solution to all the major problems, in fact the company should try one or another way to make their business or try out some other industry on the base of their good will."

- "It's beginning to feel a lot like Alice In Wonderland, as the absurdity of what is happening in Washington, and within the boardrooms of corporate America, reaches new heights.
And the tragedy of it all is the undercurrent of blackmail that exists within each of these nightmares - they're too big to fail, too many will lose their jobs, the economy will suffer - and all because of a total lack of insight and leadership. Tis a sad day in America!"
- "Author: CPL
Are corporations totally DERANGED? This does not make sense to me. If you need money to bail out your company, traveling on the private jet and continuing to collect multi million-dollar salaries, is NOT THE WAY TO GO."

Dean Goodluck

www.worldculturepictorial.com/blog/archive/all/2008/12/13

Soldier's Engagement Ring

I'll be gone to the battlefield
Don't cry, my darling
Just return to me our engagement ring

I'll be gone to the battlefield
Don't wait for me long, my darling
Just hand me our engagement ring

Remember me yet you're free
I'll ever hold the pair of rings
To my heart as I'm holding you now, my darling

I'll be gone to the battlefield
Don't cry, Don't cry, my darling
Just return to me our engagement ring

Four Steps Wiser - WcP Reading & Reflection Vol. 04

2008/12/13
WcP.Poetic.Thought

Lyrical Poem
"Soldier's Engagement Ring"

I'll be gone to the battlefield
Don't cry, my darling
Just return to me our engagement ring

I'll be gone to the battlefield
Don't wait for me long, my darling
Just hand me our engagement ring

Remember me yet you're free
I'll ever hold the pair of rings
To my heart as I'm holding you now,
my darling

I'll be gone to the battlefield
Don't cry. Don't cry, my darling
Just return to me our engagement ring

- LuCxeed

Dean Goodluck

2008/12/14
WCP.Philosophy

It was darkness which produced the lamp. It was fog that produced the compass.

"It was darkness which produced the lamp. It was fog that produced the compass."
- Victor Hugo

www.worldculturepictorial.com/blog/archive/all/2008/12/14

Reader Comments

- "Sad that situations have to get so bad before people take action. Hopefully we can turn this dynamic around and make a more concerted effort when we recognize that a problem exists. We've know about the problems with our oil supply for over 30 years."

2008/12/15
WcP.Observer

Fleet of 170
emission zero

Modec electric vans in UK: FedEx Express' fleet of >170 hybrid electric vehicles - zero tailpipe emission

www.worldculturepictorial.com/blog/archive/all/2008/12/15

Reader Comments

- "The Modec electric commercial vehicles are a really good investment since companies like FedEx are driving around town all day in order to deliver letters and packages. It is crucial to take a measure that will protect your drivers and the environment too."
- "The problem with battery powered vehicles is their driving range, but for short trips inside the city they make a great alternative to fuel-based engines, and they keep the air much cleaner."

Dean Goodluck

2008/12/16
WCP.Scientific.Mind

Orbital inclination: 51.64 degrees
Orbital speed: 7.67 km/s
Orbital period: 92.49 minutes
Orbits per day: 15.54

Zarya, 1st launched module of International Space Station (ISS), lifted into orbit 10 years ago on 20 Nov 1998

www.worldculturepictorial.com/blog/archive/all/2008/12/16

Four Steps Wiser - WcP Reading & Reflection Vol. 04

2008/12/17
WcP.Movie.Critic

Movie Critic father's humour rescues daughter

Movie. Tagline of Goya's Ghosts - "Tell me what the truth is". Do you believe truth confessed under torture?

www.worldculturepictorial.com/blog/archive/all/2008/12/17

Dean Goodluck

2008/12/18
WCP.Humor

Cartoons
amazing variety arriving at hearing; newlyweds and runaway car

Cartoons: Noah's Ark - recession edition, Christmassy profit chart, senate seat for bail-bonds, and more...

www.worldculturepictorial.com/blog/archive/all/2008/12/18

Four Steps Wiser - WcP Reading & Reflection Vol. 04

2008/12/19
WcP.Story.Teller

Beauty and Quality
Zurich, Vienna, Vancouver,
Auckland, Munich, Sydney...

10 Of the best cities offering quality life measured by traffic congestion, air quality, and personal safety

www.worldculturepictorial.com/blog/archive/all/2008/12/19

Reader Comments

(not in chronological order)
- "It was a pleasure to know the best cities across the world who are working hard to fulfill all the quality measures. One surprising thing is most of the cities are my favorite travel spots."
- "Just returned form Brussels. It really is an amazing European city."
- "Sydney, Australia is far best among this list, it has rich history, great mountains, rivers, lakes... makes city more beautiful."

- "Anyway, I believe that an apartment in Edmonton will still be the greatest! Don't you think? I mean.. I fell in love with that place!"
- "Very interesting article. Keep posting."
- "It's a unique place, and everyone's dream land. I have heard that the most costly stuff to buy here is furniture like tables and doors, they seem to be out of the ordinary."
- "It is interesting to see how people choose their holiday destination in terms of popularity and not thinking about safety and wellness standards offered in the place."
- "It looks like Switzerland is at the top of the list when it comes to quality of life. Education and air quality are rather important..."
- "Among these, Auckland is the great city, weather is perfect almost all year over there. This city has huge kind of malls, best rivers in the world, best climate."
- "I couldn't agree more!"
- "Only from what I've seen in the pictures above I wanna live in these cities. In these days the quality of air is very important for our health."
- "I really enjoyed reading your article. I found this an informative and interesting post, so I think it is very useful and knowledgeable. I'd like to thank you for the effort you've made."

- "I have been to Auckland, New Zealand and Vienna, Austria. I totally agree with you that authorities over there take care of traffic quite well and other places amongst these I am looking forward to visit are Copenhagen and Sydney."
- "Vienna has topped the list for the past five years. Cities around the world are measured on a point-scoring index against New York City, which is given a base score of 100. This year, New York was ranked 49, just behind Washington, D.C. and Chicago, which are tied for No. 45."
- "Thanks for your sharing."
- "The post about the World's finest cities that offer quality life proved to be a good read. The post helped me to compare the standard of living at different parts of the world. Keep on sharing more and more posts like this."
- "I like reading through a post that will make men and women think. Also, thanks for allowing for me to comment!"
- "Great site. I like the way you explain everything without using complicated terms."
- "Excellent post and wonderful blog, I really like this type of interesting articles, keep it up. I am really loving the theme/design of your web site."

Dean Goodluck

2008/12/20
WCP.Story.Teller

His serial number: 53310761 his income cut from $400,000 to $78 a month

Rock-and-roll star Elvis Presley drafted today in 1957 while spending Christmas at Graceland, shipped to Germany

www.worldculturepictorial.com/blog/archive/all/2008/12/20

Reader Comments

- "This really shows that you can still find folks that care about the things they post online. I really liked browsing the comments."
- "He looks very good with the pilot hat, never seen that picture before."
- "I love Elvis, he is always so handsome, attracts so many people, we remember him until today."
- "Still loving his song until today.."

- "I didn't know he was drafted in the army, I'm sure he didn't fight since they were giving preferential treatment to stars, but in their defense, these individuals were being used as a means of boosting the morale of those who actually participated in the actual war effort."
- "Elvis' army tour ended up being like a drawn out publicity campaign while at the same time becoming a sort of holiday for him away from the music industry and recharge himself. Not many get such special treatment, and he was definitely unique."
- "I agree, his time away from the music industry was a good thing. Gave him time to mature all the while, Col. Tom Parker kept him in the public's mind. Genius!"
- "Thank you for sharing good knowledge and information it's very helpful and understanding.. as we are looking for this information since long time. Regards."
- "This wonderful article on popular rock and roll star Elvis Presley lets us know more about him. There is personal information on Elvis that all would love to know. I enjoyed reading the article. The photos of Elvis are perfect showing a handsome and charming man. It's true Christmas trees are special and so are songs of Elvis."

- "Well he is a one man show.."
- "Oh yeah... No Christmas is complete without songs from Elvis Presley...Here's my list of rock songs..."
- "I enjoyed reading the article."
- "I just added your site to my favorites. I really enjoy reading your posts. Thanks!"
- "It's really great and helpful post here. Thanks for sharing with us."
- "I must admit that the article is quite good and the photos are interesting, too! Thank you for the update!"
- "This is an excellent post you have done here."
- "Hello! I've been following your current web site with regard to some time now and finally received the bravery to go in advance in addition to supply you with a howl out from Atascocita Texas!"
- "This is the article I was searching for a long time and now found it here, I enjoy this precious post and also would like to say thanks to you for such an informative post."
- "You have done very impressive work."
- "Great Post... Nice share for me, maybe nice for all readers of your post.. thanks."

- "I do not even understand how I finished up right here, but I thought this to be great. I do not recognise who you are however certainly you are going to a famous blogger for those who are not already. Cheers!"
- "First time visiting this site. It is totally tremendous because all are so nice posts. I really appreciate this. great post...!!!"
- "I actually like to recommend your pages to my other friends. You have a very captivating layout and useful ideas which I appreciate the most."
- "Professional style of writing. You have made it in such a way that the readers may understand easily."
- "Good work! Your post is an excellent example of why I keep coming back to read your excellent quality content."

Dean Goodluck

2008/12/21
WcP.Art

LuCxeed Photography
Into Shape

www.worldculturepictorial.com/blog/archive/all/2008/12/21

Reader Comments

- "This is awesome! Your photos are perfectly taken! It captured the decisive moment. I am a fan already."
- "This is absolutely fantastic photography. I recommended to lovers of photography."
- "Nice image. I love nature photography.."
- "You are a good photographer, your photography is good, you click very nice shots which are very attractive and beautiful, keep it up."
- "Beautiful pick the photo shot when I was a child a lot of pictures taken of different things. Now is also my favorite photograph list."
- "Photography is more than a hobby nowadays, it's become a trend and passion to give some awesome photo shoot, in this photo he's trying to capture nature."
- "That's great you are inspired from Photography."
- "I like this photography. These photographs are so nice."
- "Impressive capture. Awesome, very deep imagination."

- "Nice one. Which camera is used here. You could have also added the details about the aperture and the lens type you used for this. Anyway, its so cool. Perfect. Post more of your clicks."
- "I always take pleasure in your articles. You have a gift for discussing such stirring topics in ingenious yet amusing ways. Your posts help us realize that our troubles are typical, and we can solve them in ready to lend a hand ways..."
- "Magnificent web blog! This is your superb consideration and appreciate your notion with this matter. Thanks a lot for sharing!"
- "Undoubtedly enjoyed this blog! You set the subject content with exceptional abilities and a bit on the right track."
- "Some truly nice and useful info on this internet site, as well I conceive the style and design has got great features."
- "I was searching for worthy articles and this is best for me as I got many worthy information."
- "Thanks for sharing and keep writing! This is important indeed and exactly meets my need."
- "The content is incredibly useful and to be learned here. It's superb for me!"
- "It's good to read your post again! It really makes with well-thought perception and made me think differently."

Four Steps Wiser - WcP Reading & Reflection Vol. 04

2008/12/22
WcP.Common.Sense

Chico
Standing forest

Brazil's plan bears vision of forest protector shot to death 20 years ago trying to save the Amazon rain forest

www.worldculturepictorial.com/blog/archive/all/2008/12/22

Dean Goodluck

2008/12/23
WcP.Observer

Bottom line

Tough economic times. Vancouver 2010 Olympic organizers consider to cancel evening award ceremonies, $18.5-million party

www.worldculturepictorial.com/blog/archive/all/2008/12/23

Four Steps Wiser - WcP Reading & Reflection Vol. 04

2008/12/24
WcP.Humor

In the season of Joy

President Kennedy feeding a deer.
Next morning wonders why no toast at breakfast, told he fed entire supply to deer

www.worldculturepictorial.com/blog/archive/all/2008/12/24

Dean Goodluck

2008/12/25
WCP.Story.Teller

1659 ~ 1681
Christmas outlawed

Once upon a time: Christmas celebration outlawed in Boston; anyone exhibiting Christmas spirit fined 5 shillings

www.worldculturepictorial.com/blog/archive/all/2008/12/25

Reader Comments

- "Christmas is both a sacrosanct religious occasion and an overall social and business marvel. For two centuries, individuals around the globe have been watching it with conventions and practices that are both religious and mainstream in nature. Christians observe Christmas Day as the commemoration of the introduction of Jesus of Nazareth, an otherworldly pioneer whose lessons frame the premise of their religion."

- "You are doing an amazing job."
- "Christmas is the time of enjoyment and it is the day when you think about the good and bad deeds. It is the day when you strongly decide to work good deeds so that people appreciate or recognize you. Your article is so amazing in which you mention all the history of Christmas."
- "Christmas is the name of the celebration in which you feel happy and it is all about love. The love for Jesus Christ and reminder of good deeds. It is the day when you decorate your whole house and street."
- "Christmas is a time to celebrate with family and friends and show their love for God. It is the time to remind the memory of birth of Jesus Christ and do something good for better life and help each other. But it is the great history of the Christmas and I feel amazing."
- "Good to read :)"
- "This blog gives history of the Christmas. I have heard lots of things about the event of Christmas which comes every year in December. This is good information which helps me lots."

- "Christmas is an event in which every person can enjoy in specific ways. The season has religious importance and everybody celebrates this event with family and completes all the conditions to celebrate this event. This post is areligious and worthy to me because it has the history related to Christmas and I want to know about this event. And it's passion of my life."
- "Christmas is the event in which we celebrate with full of spirit and courage. When Christmas comes it means it's time to rejoice and full of fun. We should learn about the history so that we know about our ancestors and how how they celebrated Christmas. The article is very good."
- "Christmas is the best celebration that everyone enjoys with best methods but here I find Christmas spirit fined 5 shillings that helps me a lot to understand this topic. This website is the best way of providing great knowledge to complete the task."

Four Steps Wiser - WcP Reading & Reflection Vol. 04

2008/12/26
WcP.Publisher

Think Ahead
"To a Greener Earth"

www.worldculturepictorial.com/blog/archive/all/2008/12/26

Dean Goodluck

2009 — To a Greener Earth

©2008 D'Moon ♦ ThinkAhead™ Calendar ♦   www.worldculturepictorial.com

Four Steps Wiser - WcP Reading & Reflection Vol. 04

2008/12/26
WcP.Publisher

ThinkAhead™ Calendar
vision in visuals

"If 'Habit is the nursery of errors', let ThinkAhead™ Calendar be the nursery of greatness.

ThinkAhead™ Calendar is vision in visuals, visual vision.
Nature tosses lives into the constant flow of time.
Think ahead for Life ahead. Vision delivers options to embrace the near future with choices.

The traditional calendar presents dates based on the position of the sun.
The planner is more about "planning" events, schedules by the hour.
ThinkAhead™ Calendar is a visual presentation of your own vision, choices for a better life in a better world, to mark inspired ideas for the near future on the seasonally-renewed always-12-months-ahead calendar.

Dean Goodluck

2009 — To a Greener Earth

January	February	March
April	May	June
July	August	September
October	November	December

©2008 D'Moon ◆ ThinkAhead™ Calendar ◆

www.worldculturepictorial.com

Four Steps Wiser - WcP Reading & Reflection Vol. 04

Destiny is a mystery.
Embrace the near future
with choices you make.
Think ahead for Life ahead.
It would be our blessing when
ThinkAhead™ Calendar contributes
to the habit of thinking ahead,
for better lives in a better world.

Here is the first release with themes:
'To a Greener Earth'
and
"For kids, the future of our World'."

www.worldculturepictorial.com/blog/archive/all/2008/12/26

Reader Comments

- "Very colourful calendar with nice messages on them."
- "This is so cool. If "Habit is the nursery of errors", let ThinkAhead™ Calendar be the nursery of greatness.' "

Dean Goodluck

Four Steps Wiser - WcP Reading & Reflection Vol. 04

To a Greener Earth 2010

Dean Goodluck

2008/12/27
WCP.Philosophy

*Intellectuals solve problems;
geniuses prevent them.*

"Intellectuals solve problems;
geniuses prevent them."
- Albert Einstein

www.worldculturepictorial.com/blog/archive/all/2008/12/27

Reader Comments

- "The sad realization is that we experienced a lack of both intellectuals and geniuses in Washington for the past eight years. Based on the first selections to head up the new administration's efforts to combat climate change and the energy crisis, that dynamic is about to change."

Four Steps Wiser - WcP Reading & Reflection Vol. 04

2008/12/28
WcP.Story.Teller

2,600 BC:
2,300,000 2.5-ton blocks of stone

World's tallest buildings (part i):
Cheops Pyramid, Lincoln Cathedral,
St. Olav, Strasbourg Cathedral, St. Nikolai

www.worldculturepictorial.com/blog/archive/all/2008/12/28

Reader Comments

◆ "You might be astounded that the title of the world's tallest structure does not change hands that regularly. Actually, just 19 man-influenced structures have at any point held the title all through our history, a shocking actuality when you understand what number of tall structures have been built in the course of the last five thousand years."

- "In summer, castles are crowded with tourists, however, you will be offered interesting entertainment, such as light-music performances or night walks through illuminated gardens and parks. In addition, flowering flower beds and gardens make this season more attractive than a visit in the winter."
- "The buildings are beautiful. I love the way historical cities look. I even couldn't help to mention it in my last assignment. Impressive and encouraging."
- "There is no universal definition for the word beauty. Beauty, as they say, is in the eye of the beholder. Beautiful is your canvas on which to paint."
- "The article surely contains some useful details on different places and of course the world's tallest buildings. Anyone can get a brief but clean idea about the places specified here and this is very informative for travel purposes."
- "Egyptian Pyramids are well known and a good place to visit, St. Olav is the third highest as suggested here and this is because the sharp edges as seen in the picture. All the buildings are different in looks and thanks for sharing the article and information related to this."

- "Buildings like these have made us famous overseas, so we should be grateful to architects for giving us these impressive constructions."
- "These are indeed some of the greatest buildings ever made, that somehow remained in a good shape for all these years. Many of them are part of restoration programs and architects will be able to preserve them, so that people can visit these architectural gems for many years to come."
- "The historical backdrop of development, Britain is entirely far down. In the entire western world, the Greeks were likely the most persuasive human advancement. English individuals are in some cases so pleased with themselves that they look silly."
- "I have actually been to Cheops pyramid and the feeling is like none other. It is vast, glorious, admirable and out of this world. I have read that the pyramid is so big that if it were an household place literally thousands of people could live in it. The other places mentioned in here are also great and it is really good to know how there is a constant evolution of designs and how artisans made these places look fantastic. The great thing about it is, that these places are still great to watch and people marvel at the gigantic nature of these constructions."

Dean Goodluck

- "Interesting article! Never knew that cathedral owners in the past were so fixated on building the tallest building. Was there a particular reason why they had to outdo each other in terms of height? Still, those structures are grand looking even today."
- "I want to go there in person! The world is beautiful!"
- "Good article, I love high buildings especially old, after this article we dream of being in all these buildings."
- "Great post! A fantastic summary/overview. Thanks for the work! Keep going!"
- "Excellent post, great pictures :)"

Four Steps Wiser - WcP Reading & Reflection Vol. 04

2008/12/29
WcP.Publisher

*"For Kids
the Future of Our World"*

www.worldculturepictorial.com/blog/archive/all/2008/12/29

Dean Goodluck

2008/12/30
WCP.Publisher

*"Unburned Bridge
for Wisdom to Walk on"
by LuCxeed*

"Love speaks for Romance, Love speaks more for Compassion." New book release. A gift, inspirational and motivational

"The poems are wide-ranging in topics,
many inspired by true events,
by true stories while alongside,
photographs and art, by nature.
Poetry from life is presented to Life -
inviting readers to enjoy
Poem in Art, Poetry in Gallery,
voice and visual art under one roof.
Each page delivers a surprise,
refreshing and appealing."

www.worldculturepictorial.com/blog/archive/all/2008/12/30

Four Steps Wiser - WcP Reading & Reflection Vol. 04

2008/12/31
WcP.Story.Teller

39 countries on all 7 continents dance with Matt

"Thank you for dancing with me!"
Matt invited people in 39 countries on all 7 continents to come out and dance...

www.worldculturepictorial.com/blog/archive/all/2008/12/31

Robert Louis Stevenson

"Wine is bottled poetry."

Let's toast

Leisure reading along the journey of publishing this book

Dean Goodluck

jealousy

He must feel blooded with the spirit of a god
to sit opposite you and listen, and reply,
to your talk, your laughter, your touching,
breath-held silences. But what I feel, sitting here
and watching you, so stops my heart and binds
my tongue that I can't think what I might say
to breach the aureole around you there.
It's as if someone with flint and stone had sparked
a fire that kindled the flesh along my arms
and smothered me in its smoke-blind rush.
Paler than summer grass, it seems
I am already dead, or little short of it

— Sappho

Four Steps Wiser - WcP Reading & Reflection Vol. 04

Poem in Art
Jealousy
Sappho

He must feel blooded with the spirit of a god
to sit opposite you and listen, and reply,
to your talk, your laughter, your touching,
breath-held silences. But what I feel, sitting here
and watching you, so stops my heart and binds
my tongue that I can't think what I might say
to breach the aureole around you there.
It's as if someone with flint and stone had sparked
a fire that kindled the flesh along my arms
and smothered me in its smoke-blind rush.
Paler than summer grass, it seems
I am already dead, or little short of dying.

- Jealousy
by Sappho

Dean Goodluck

a strange wild song

Poem
A Strange Wild Song
Lewis Carroll

He thought he saw an Elephant
That practised on a fife:
He looked again, and found it was
A letter from his wife.
'At length I realize,' he said,
'The bitterness of life! '

He thought he saw a Buffalo
Upon the chimney-piece:
He looked again, and found it was
His Sister's Husband's Niece.
'Unless you leave this house,' he said,
'I'll send for the police! '

He thought he saw a Rattlesnake
That questioned him in Greek:
He looked again, and found it was
The Middle of Next Week.
'The one thing I regret,' he said,
'Is that it cannot speak! '

Dean Goodluck

He thought he saw a Banker's Clerk
Descending from the bus:
He looked again, and found it was
A Hippopotamus.
'If this should stay to dine,' he said,
'There won't be much for us!'

He thought he saw a Kangaroo
That worked a Coffee-mill:
He looked again, and found it was
A Vegetable-Pill.
'Were I to swallow this,' he said,
'I should be very ill!'

He thought he saw a Coach-and-Four
That stood beside his bed:
He looked again, and found it was
A Bear without a Head.
'Poor thing,' he said, 'poor silly thing!
It's waiting to be fed!'

He thought he saw an Albatross
That fluttered round the lamp:
He looked again, and found it was
A Penny-Postage Stamp.
'You'd best be getting home,' he said:
'The nights are very damp!'

He thought he saw a Garden-Door
That opened with a key:
He looked again, and found it was
A Double Rule of Three:
'And all its mystery,' he said,
'Is clear as day to me!'

He thought he saw a Argument
That proved he was the Pope:
He looked again, and found it was
A Bar of Mottled Soap.
'A fact so dread,' he faintly said,
'Extinguishes all hope!'

- A Strange Wild Song
by Lewis Carroll

Dean Goodluck

William Cullen Bryant

The Arctic Lover

Gone is the long, long winter night;
Look, my beloved one!
How glorious, through his depths of light,
Rolls the majestic sun!
The willows, waked from winter's death,
Give out a fragrance like thy breath--
The summer is begun!
......
See, love, my boat is moored for thee,
By ocean's weedy floor--
The petrel does not skim the sea
More swiftly than my oar.
We'll go, where, on the rocky isles,
Her eggs the screaming sea-fowl piles
Beside the pebbly shore.

Four Steps Wiser - WcP Reading & Reflection Vol. 04

Poem in Art
The Arctic Lover
William Cullen Bryant

Gone is the long, long winter night;
Look, my beloved one!
How glorious, through his depths of light,
Rolls the majestic sun!
The willows, waked from winter's death,
Give out a fragrance like thy breath--
The summer is begun!

...
See, love, my boat is moored for thee,
By ocean's weedy floor--
The petrel does not skim the sea
More swiftly than my oar.
We'll go, where, on the rocky isles,
Her eggs the screaming sea-fowl piles
Beside the pebbly shore.

- from The Arctic Lover
by William Cullen Bryant

Dean Goodluck

the Arrow and the Song

Four Steps Wiser - WcP Reading & Reflection Vol. 04

Poem
The Arrow And The Song
Henry Wadsworth Longfellow

I shot an arrow into the air,
It fell to earth, I knew not where;
For, so swiftly it flew, the sight
Could not follow it in its flight.

I breathed a song into the air,
It fell to earth, I knew not where;
For who has sight so keen and strong,
That it can follow the flight of song?

Long, long afterward, in an oak
I found the arrow, still unbroke;
And the song, from beginning to end,
I found again in the heart of a friend.

- The Arrow And The Song
by Henry Wadsworth Longfellow

Dean Goodluck

Paradise Lost

Poem
Paradise Lost: Book 01
(lines 544-654)
John Milton

All in a moment through the gloom were seen
Ten thousand banners rise into the air,
With orient colours waving: with them rose
A forest huge of spears; and thronging helms
Appeared, and serried shields in thick array
Of depth immeasurable. Anon they move
In perfect phalanx to the Dorian mood
Of flutes and soft recorders--such as raised
To height of noblest temper heroes old
Arming to battle, and instead of rage
Deliberate valour breathed, firm, and unmoved
With dread of death to flight or foul retreat;
Nor wanting power to mitigate and swage
With solemn touches troubled thoughts, and chase
Anguish and doubt and fear and sorrow and pain
From mortal or immortal minds. Thus they,
Breathing united force with fixed thought,
Moved on in silence to soft pipes that charmed
Their painful steps o'er the burnt soil. And now
Advanced in view they stand--a horrid front

Dean Goodluck

Of dreadful length and dazzling arms, in guise
Of warriors old, with ordered spear and shield,
Awaiting what command their mighty Chief
Had to impose. He through the armed files
Darts his experienced eye, and soon traverse
The whole battalion views--their order due,
Their visages and stature as of gods;
Their number last he sums. And now his heart
Distends with pride, and, hardening in his strength,
Glories: for never, since created Man,
Met such embodied force as, named with these,
Could merit more than that small infantry
Warred on by cranes--though all the giant brood
Of Phlegra with th' heroic race were joined
That fought at Thebes and Ilium, on each side
Mixed with auxiliar gods; and what resounds
In fable or romance of Uther's son,
Begirt with British and Armoric knights;
And all who since, baptized or infidel,
Jousted in Aspramont, or Montalban,
Damasco, or Marocco, or Trebisond,
Or whom Biserta sent from Afric shore
When Charlemain with all his peerage fell
By Fontarabbia. Thus far these beyond

Compare of mortal prowess, yet observed
Their dread Commander. He, above the rest
In shape and gesture proudly eminent,
Stood like a tower. His form had yet not lost
All her original brightness, nor appeared
Less than Archangel ruined, and th' excess
Of glory obscured: as when the sun new-risen
Looks through the horizontal misty air
Shorn of his beams, or, from behind the moon,
In dim eclipse, disastrous twilight sheds
On half the nations, and with fear of change
Perplexes monarchs. Darkened so, yet shone
Above them all th' Archangel: but his face
Deep scars of thunder had intrenched, and care
Sat on his faded cheek, but under brows
Of dauntless courage, and considerate pride
Waiting revenge. Cruel his eye, but cast
Signs of remorse and passion, to behold
The fellows of his crime, the followers rather
(Far other once beheld in bliss) condemned
For ever now to have their lot in pain--
Millions of Spirits for his fault amerced
Of Heaven, and from eternal splendours flung
For his revolt--yet faithful how they stood,

Dean Goodluck

Their glory withered; as, when heaven's fire
Hath scathed the forest oaks or mountain pines,
With singed top their stately growth, though bare,
Stands on the blasted heath. He now prepared
To speak; whereat their doubled ranks they bend
From wing to wing, and half enclose him round
With all his peers: attention held them mute.
Thrice he assayed, and thrice, in spite of scorn,
Tears, such as Angels weep, burst forth: at last
Words interwove with sighs found out their way:--
"O myriads of immortal Spirits! O Powers
Matchless, but with th' Almighth!--and that strife
Was not inglorious, though th' event was dire,
As this place testifies, and this dire change,
Hateful to utter. But what power of mind,
Forseeing or presaging, from the depth
Of knowledge past or present, could have feared
How such united force of gods, how such
As stood like these, could ever know repulse?
For who can yet believe, though after loss,
That all these puissant legions, whose exile
Hath emptied Heaven, shall fail to re-ascend,
Self-raised, and repossess their native seat?
For me, be witness all the host of Heaven,

Four Steps Wiser - WcP Reading & Reflection Vol. 04

If counsels different, or danger shunnedBy me,
have lost our hopes. But he who reigns
Monarch in Heaven till then as one secure
Sat on his throne, upheld by old repute,
Consent or custom, and his regal state
Put forth at full, but still his strength concealed--
Which tempted our attempt, and wrought our fall.
Henceforth his might we know, and know our own,
So as not either to provoke, or dread
New war provoked: our better part remains
To work in close design, by fraud or guile,
What force effected not; that he no less
At length from us may find, who overcomes
By force hath overcome but half his foe.
Space may produce new Worlds; whereof so rife
There went a fame in Heaven that he ere long
Intended to create, and therein plant
A generation whom his choice regard
Should favour equal to the Sons of Heaven.

- from Paradise Lost: Book 01 (lines 544-654)
by John Milton

Dean Goodluck

Speech: "Friends, Romans, countrymen, lend me your ears"

Four Steps Wiser - WcP Reading & Reflection Vol. 04

Poem
Speech:
"Friends, Romans, countrymen, lend me your ears"
William Shakespeare

Friends, Romans, countrymen, lend me your ears;
I come to bury Caesar, not to praise him.
The evil that men do lives after them;
The good is oft interred with their bones;
So let it be with Caesar. The noble Brutus
Hath told you Caesar was ambitious:
If it were so, it was a grievous fault,
And grievously hath Caesar answer'd it.
Here, under leave of Brutus and the rest-
For Brutus is an honourable man;
So are they all, all honourable men-
Come I to speak in Caesar's funeral.
He was my friend, faithful and just to me:
But Brutus says he was ambitious;
And Brutus is an honourable man.
He hath brought many captives home to Rome
Whose ransoms did the general coffers fill:
Did this in Caesar seem ambitious?

Dean Goodluck

When that the poor have cried, Caesar hath wept:
Ambition should be made of sterner stuff:
Yet Brutus says he was ambitious;
And Brutus is an honourable man.
You all did see that on the Lupercal
I thrice presented him a kingly crown,
Which he did thrice refuse: was this ambition?
Yet Brutus says he was ambitious;
And, sure, he is an honourable man.
I speak not to disprove what Brutus spoke,
But here I am to speak what I do know.
You all did love him once, not without cause:
What cause withholds you then, to mourn for him?

Four Steps Wiser - WcP Reading & Reflection Vol. 04

O judgment! thou art fled to brutish beasts,
And men have lost their reason. Bear with me;
My heart is in the coffin there with Caesar,
And I must pause till it come back to me.

- Speech:
"Friends, Romans, countrymen,
lend me your ears"
by William Shakespeare

Publisher's Blog:
WcP Blog | World Culture Pictorial
www.worldculturepictorial.com

"Extraordinary stuff,
just basically astonishing!
Keep it up in future.
I am truly inspired by this site!"
- Anonymous

"I was so impressed by it
I felt I would reach out to you
to say thank you. Great work...
that's one great blog you've got there!"
- Kayla

"Thanks for trying to
make the world a better place."
- Anonymous

Dean Goodluck

Other Volumes in the Series

full color print
through and through
including art images

www.worldculturepictorial.com/one-step-wiser.html

Four Steps Wiser - WcP Reading & Reflection Vol. 04

Other Volumes in the Series

full color print
through and through
including art images

www.worldculturepictorial.com/one-step-wiser.html

Dean Goodluck

Other Volumes in the Series

b&w interior print
on classic creme paper
including art images

www.worldculturepictorial.com/one-step-wiser.html

Four Steps Wiser - WcP Reading & Reflection Vol. 04

www.ingramcontent.com/pod-product-compliance
Lightning Source LLC
Chambersburg PA
CBHW041324110526
44592CB00021B/2810